THE EVOLUTION
OF AFRICA'S MAJOR NATIONS

Sierra Leone

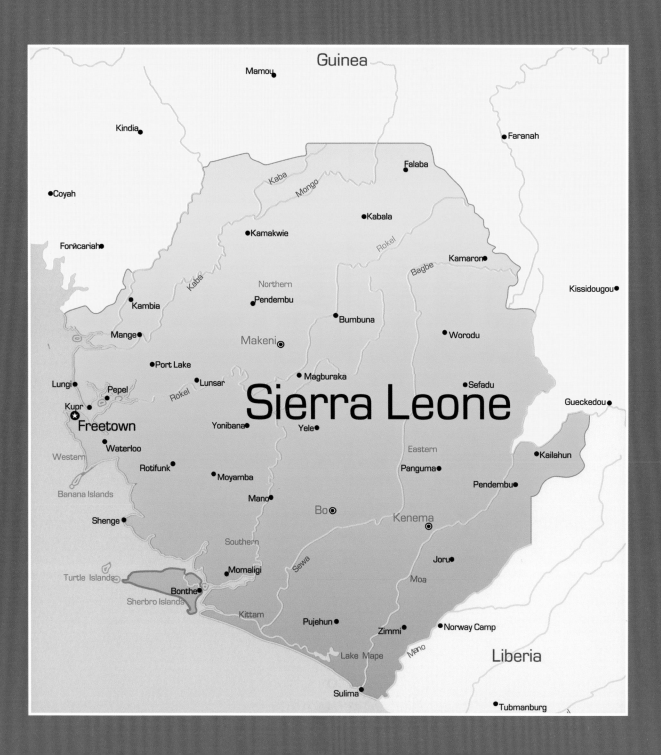

THE EVOLUTION
OF AFRICA'S MAJOR NATIONS

Sierra Leone

Judy Hasday

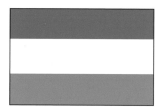

Mason Crest
Philadelphia

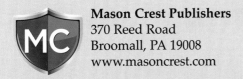

Mason Crest Publishers
370 Reed Road
Broomall, PA 19008
www.masoncrest.com

CPSIA Compliance Information: Batch #EAMN2013-21. For further information,
contact Mason Crest Publishers at 1-866-MCP-Book.

First printing

1 3 5 7 9 8 6 4 2

Library of Congress Cataloging-in-Publication Data

Hasday, Judy L., 1957-
Sierra Leone / Judy Hasday.
    p. cm. — (Evolution of Africa's major nations.)
Includes bibliographical references and index.
ISBN 978-1-4222-2202-7 (hardcover)
ISBN 978-1-4222-2230-0 (pbk.)
ISBN 978-1-4222-9442-0 (ebook)
1. Sierra Leone—Juvenile literature. I. Title. II. Series: Evolution of Africa's major nations.
DT516.18.H37 2012
966.4—dc22
                          2011018506

Table of Contents

Africa: Progress, Problems, and Promise

Robert I. Rotberg

Africa is the cradle of humankind, but for millennia it was off the familiar, beaten path of global commerce and discovery. Its many peoples therefore developed largely apart from the diffusion of modern knowledge and the spread of technological innovation until the 17th through 19th centuries. With the coming to Africa of the book, the wheel, the hoe, and the modern rifle and cannon, foreigners also brought the vastly destructive transatlantic slave trade, oppression, discrimination, and onerous colonial rule. Emerging from that crucible of European rule, Africans created nationalistic movements and then claimed their numerous national independences in the 1960s. The result is the world's largest continental assembly of new countries.

There are 53 members of the African Union, a regional political grouping, and 48 of those nations lie south of the Sahara. Fifteen of them, including mighty Ethiopia, are landlocked, making international trade and economic growth that much more arduous and expensive. Access to navigable rivers is limited, natural harbors are few, soils are poor and thin, several countries largely consist of miles and miles of sand, and tropical diseases have sapped the strength and productivity of innumerable millions. Being landlocked, having few resources (although countries along Africa's west coast have tapped into deep offshore petroleum and gas reservoirs), and being beset by malaria, tuberculosis, schistosomiasis, AIDS, and many other maladies has kept much of Africa poor for centuries.

Thirty-two of the world's poorest 44 countries are African. Hunger is common. So is rapid deforestation and desertification. Unemployment rates are often over 50 percent, for jobs are few—even in agriculture. Where Africa once

Wearing traditional garb, Sierra Leoneans perform a dance on a street in Freetown.

was a land of small villages and a few large cities, with almost everyone engaged in growing grain or root crops or grazing cattle, camels, sheep, and goats, today more than half of all the more than 1 billion Africans, especially those who live south of the Sahara, reside in towns and cities. Traditional agriculture hardly pays, and a number of countries in Africa—particularly the smaller and more fragile ones—can no longer feed themselves.

There is not one Africa, for the continent is full of contradictions and variety. Of the 750 million people living south of the Sahara, at least 150 million live in Nigeria, 85 million in Ethiopia, 68 million in the Democratic Republic of the Congo, and 49 million in South Africa. By contrast, tiny Djibouti and Equatorial Guinea have fewer than 1 million people each, and prosperous Botswana and Namibia each are under 2.2 million in population. Within some countries, even medium-sized ones like Zambia (12 million), there are a plethora of distinct ethnic groups speaking separate languages. Zambia, typical with its multitude of competing entities, has 70 such peoples, roughly broken down

Workers search for gems in diamond fields outside Freetown, Sierra Leone.

into four language and cultural zones. Three of those languages jostle with English for primacy.

Given the kaleidoscopic quality of African culture and deep-grained poverty, it is no wonder that Africa has developed economically and politically less rapidly than other regions. Since independence from colonial rule, weak governance has also plagued Africa and contributed significantly to the widespread poverty of its peoples. Only Botswana and offshore Mauritius have been governed democratically without interruption since independence. Both are among Africa's wealthiest countries, too, thanks to the steady application of good governance.

Aside from those two nations, and South Africa, Africa has been a continent of coups since 1960, with massive and oil-rich Nigeria suffering incessant periods of harsh, corrupt, autocratic military rule. Nearly every other country on or around the continent, small and large, has been plagued by similar bouts of instability and dictatorial rule. In the 1970s and 1980s Idi Amin ruled Uganda capriciously and Jean-Bedel Bokassa proclaimed himself emperor of the Central African Republic. Macias Nguema of Equatorial Guinea was another in that same mold. More recently Daniel arap Moi held Kenya in thrall and Robert Mugabe has imposed himself on once-prosperous Zimbabwe. In both of those cases, as in the case of Gnassingbe Eyadema in Togo and the late Mobutu Sese Seko in Congo, these presidents stole wildly and drove entire peoples and their nations into penury. Corruption is common in Africa, and so are a weak rule-of-law framework, misplaced development, high expenditures on soldiers and low expenditures on health and education, and a widespread (but not universal) refusal on the part of leaders to work well for their followers and citizens.

Conflict between groups within countries has also been common in Africa. More than 12 million Africans have been killed in civil wars since 1990, while another 9 million have become refugees. Decades of conflict in Sudan led to a January 2011 referendum in which the people of southern Sudan voted overwhelmingly to secede and form a new state. In early 2011, anti-government protests spread throughout North Africa, ultimately toppling long-standing regimes in Tunisia and Egypt. That same year, there were serious ongoing hostilities within Chad, Ivory Coast, Libya, the Niger Delta region of Nigeria, and Somalia.

Despite such dangers, despotism, and decay, Africa is improving. Botswana and Mauritius, now joined by South Africa, Senegal, Kenya, and Ghana, are beacons of democratic growth and enlightened rule. Uganda and Senegal are taking the lead in combating and reducing the spread of AIDS, and others are following. There are serious signs of the kinds of progressive economic policy changes that might lead to prosperity for more of Africa's peoples. The trajectory in Africa is positive.

(Opposite) The sun sets over Lakka Beach, near Freetown. (Right) In this view of fishing trawlers on the Atlantic Ocean, the mountains of Sierra Leone can be seen looming over the shoreline.

A Diamond in the Rough

KUSHE! OW DI BODI? That's how Sierra Leoneans would greet you, offering a welcome and asking how you are, in **Krio**. It is the language spoken by most people in the country, regardless of their ethnic background. One of the smallest countries in Africa, Sierra Leone is a land graced with picturesque beaches and lush rain forests, a large natural harbor, and abundant diamond mines. However, it also has a dark and painful history of violence, pain, and suffering from more than 10 years of a brutal civil war. There is now peace in this country, and with its rich resources and natural beauty, Sierra Leone offers promise of a brighter future for its 6 million citizens.

Most of the Republic of Sierra Leone is located on the west coast "hump" of Africa, the second-largest continent on earth. Sierra Leone lies between the Tropic of Cancer and the equator and is bordered by two countries—Guinea

THE GEOGRAPHY OF SIERRA LEONE

Location: Western Africa, bordering the Atlantic Ocean, between Guinea and Liberia

Area: (slightly smaller than South Carolina)
  total: 27,699 square miles (71,740 sq km)
  land: 27,653 square miles (71,620 sq km)
  water: 46 square miles (120 sq km)

Borders: Guinea, 405 miles (652 km); Liberia, 190 miles (306 km)

Climate: tropical; hot, humid

Terrain: coastal belt of mangrove swamps, wooded hill country, upland plateau, mountains in the east

Elevation extremes:
  lowest point: Atlantic Ocean, 0 feet
  highest point: Mount Bintimani (Loma Mansa), 6391 feet (1,948 m)

Natural hazards: sand and dust storms, flooding

Source: CIA World Factbook, 2011.

to the north and northeast and Liberia to the southeast. On the west and southwest the country's 210-mile (340-kilometer) coastline meets the Atlantic Ocean. Several islands, including Sherbro, Banana, and Bunce, lie just off-shore.

Sierra Leone covers 27,699 square miles (71,740 square kilometers) and is about the size of the state of South Carolina. Water is plentiful, thanks to several rivers that run from the mountainous regions in the northeastern part of the country to the southwestern lowlands, before eventually flowing into the Atlantic Ocean. These rivers provide both drinking water and a means of transportation for Sierra Leoneans traveling from one town to another. Some of the most accessible rivers include the Great and Little Scarcies, Rokel, Jong, Sewa, Mano, and Moa.

A DIVERSE TERRAIN

Despite Sierra Leone's small size, it has a diverse terrain that includes mountain ranges, mangrove swamps, and tropical shorelines. The country can be divided into four geographic regions: the *plateau* and mountains in the east, the interior plains, the Sierra Leone peninsula, and the coastal marshes. The country's unique, untamed terrain and mountains impressed Portuguese explorers who reached the region in the 15th century. They called the area *Serra Lyoa*, or "Lion Mountains."

The mountains and plateaus of Sierra Leone take up about 50 percent of the total land area. Plateaus closely encircle the mountain ranges, which

Sierra Leone's rivers transport people and goods throughout the country.

can be found in the eastern, northeastern, and southeastern parts of the country. These upland regions include the Sula-Kangari Mountains, the Tingi Hills, and the Loma Mountains. The highest elevation in Sierra Leone is in the Loma Mountains, Mount Bintumani (also known as Loma Mansa). At 6,391 feet (1,948 meters) high, Mount Bintumani is also the highest point in West Africa.

Near the town of Kenema in the southeastern part of Sierra Leone lie the Kambui Hills, where the country's rich cache of diamonds is located. This is also where the Kambui Hills Forest Reserve can be found. Home to more than 200 species of birds, as well as primates and larger mammals, the reserve is threatened by habitat destruction from illegal logging.

The interior plains region stretches inland from the Atlantic Ocean eastward through the coastal swamps to the hilly and wooded Sierra Leone Peninsula, where the capital city of Freetown is located. Its natural harbor—the third largest in the world—is Sierra Leone's chief port. As the economic center of the city, the harbor handles the majority of Freetown's exports and imports. Farther east, the inland region is dominated by *rainforests*, farmlands, and shrub-covered terrain.

ISLANDS

Just off the western coast of mainland Sierra Leone lie several small islands. The largest of them, Sherbro, features more than 65 miles (105 km) of tropical beaches. Its chief port and commercial center is the town of Bonthe. To promote tourist development of the island, the Sierra Leone government is building a new international airport on Sherbro.

Africa's past history of slavery and the slave trade is present in Sherbro and in the nearby island of Bunce. In 1815, British *abolitionists* settled 88 freed slaves on Sherbro, making it the first community of former slaves to be established in Africa. In contrast, tens of thousands of slaves passed through nearby Bunce Island, which was once the largest British slave trading post in all of West Africa. Captured Africans were exported to North America and the West Indies by way of Bunce from 1670 to 1808, when the British finally shut down the trading center. Named a national historic site in 1948, Bunce Island today is home to a number of ruins, including a factory house, slave prison, watchtowers, and storerooms.

The island's ties with the United States date back to the 1770s, when a business relationship was forged between Richard Oswald (the principal owner of Bunce Island) and Henry Laurens (a rice plantation owner and slave trader in the colony of South Carolina). As a result, numerous Africans ended up working as slaves on rice plantations in the modern-day states of South Carolina and Georgia. Today, many of the African-Americans called Gullahs, who live along the coastal regions of those two states, have *ancestral* ties to Bunce Island.

Another significant island in Sierra Leone can be found in the Moa River, which runs through the eastern part of the country. Tiwai Island, which means "Big Island" in the local Mende language, is one of the Sierra Leone's largest inland islands. Located 186 miles (300 km) from Freetown, it encompasses 4.5 square miles (12 sq km).

Many different animals live on Tiwai Island, including more than 3,000 primates, the rare pygmy hippopotamus, and more than 135 bird species. The chimpanzees that live on Tiwai exhibit advanced traits not found in other chimp populations. They have an unusual ability to use tools: they crack open nuts by using stones as hammers and tree roots as anvils.

Visitors to Tiwai can go white-water rafting on the Moa River during the rainy season. In the dry months, they can take a calmer boat or canoe ride down the river, where they may see many different species of birds flying overhead, river turtles paddling by, and otters playing on the sandy beaches.

Found in only a few West African countries, the rare pygmy hippopotamus thrives in the dense forests of the Tiwai Island Wildlife Sanctuary of Sierra Leone.

TWO MAIN SEASONS

Sierra Leone has a tropical climate, so conditions are hot and humid for most of the year. Temperatures vary little throughout the year, usually reaching 80°F (27°C) in January and 78°F (26°C) in July. There are two main seasons in Sierra Leone: rainy and dry. The rainy season runs from May to October and can bring as much as 79 inches (200 cm) of rain to the northern part of the country, and 157 inches (398 cm) of rain to the southern region. Although the rainy season is the best time for farmers to plant seeds and vegetable crops, it can also bring floods that destroy land and property.

During the dry season, which runs from November to April, a strong dusty trade wind blows down from the Sahara Desert in North Africa. As this wind, called the *harmattan*, whips across the desert, it picks up so much dust and sand particles that it reduces visibility and at times even blocks the sunlight. However, because the harmattan brings cooler air and relief from the humid, hot temperatures, is often referred to as "the Doctor."

SIERRA LEONE'S WILDLIFE

Civil war, overfarming, and hunting have caused Sierra Leone to lose much of its natural habitat, especially in the central part of the country. However, the country still contains an abundance of primates, reptiles, birds, fish, and other wildlife. Sierra Leone has 21 government-protected areas, including Outamba-Kilimi National Park, which is home to elephants, pygmy hippos, chimpanzees, sooty mangabeys, and colobus monkeys.

The rufous fishing owl is one of more than 600 species of birds in Sierra Leone. The large owl can be found along riverbanks and in mangroves in the Gola rainforests, in the southeastern part of the country.

In other areas of the country, forests and *savannas* provide habitats for a vast variety of animals, including leopards, lions, hyenas, cape buffalo, porcupines, antelope, and bush pigs. Hippopotamuses, crocodiles, manatees, and alligators swim in Sierra Leone's rivers, while a variety of sea creatures such as such as bonga (a species of herring), tuna, mackerel, lobsters, shrimp, barracuda, and sharks fill the coastal waters and streams.

The chimpanzee population in Sierra Leone has been in great decline over the past 30 years. In regions where more than 20,000 chimps once roamed freely, only about 3,000 remain today. In 1995, the Tacugama Chimp Sanctuary, located about 30 minutes north of Freetown, opened its doors to help with the rescue and rehabilitation of orphaned chimpanzees. The 100-acre sanctuary houses approximately 80 chimps.

Sierra Leone is a prime spot for bird lovers. More than 625 bird species nest along the shorelines and in the wetlands, savannas, and forests of the country. On any given day, visitors can spot a variety of plovers, sandpipers, terns, hornbills, sunbirds, parrots, owls, kingfishers, green pigeons, African magpies, and vultures. Efforts are in place in the Gola Forest Reserve, in southeastern Sierra Leone, to protect several endangered species, including the fishing owl, green-tailed bristlebill, and white-necked picathartes. The reserve is one of the last rainforest areas left in West Africa.

Slavery is part of both Sierra Leone's past and its recent history. (Opposite) Freetown was originally settled in the late 1700s by freed slaves. (Right) This young girl was enslaved in 1999 by members of the rebel group Revolutionary United Front (RUF). The rebels cut off her arm before setting her free.

2 The Colony and the Protectorate

ITS LOCATION ON THE WESTERN COAST of Africa is just one of Sierra Leone's many natural resources. Easy access by sea has brought an abundance of visitors, whose influence has made Sierra Leone the colorful, multicultural nation of peoples that it is today. However, other natural resources, particularly the country's rich diamond deposits, have caused the small nation to be pillaged, colonized, and fractured by factions fighting to control its wealth.

EARLY PEOPLES

Very little is known about the history of Sierra Leone before the 1400s, although archeological findings indicate people have lived in the area for thousands of years. Archeologists have found stone tools dating to the Late Stone Age (around the third century B.C.).

Various ethnic groups appear to have migrated to Sierra Leone's coastal region at different times, according to researchers who have studied the language patterns of the *indigenous* peoples (including the Sherbro, Krim, Temne, and Limba). Scholars believe that the Mende migrated to Sierra Leone from the western Sudan between the 2nd and 16th centuries.

Many of these ethnic groups formed chiefdoms—communities led by a chief. It was not uncommon for tribes to fight one another, usually over territory or valuable resources like food and water. As the tribes conquered one another, the people intermarried and adopted one another's customs and cultural, religious, and social beliefs.

EUROPEAN EXPLORERS ARRIVE

When European explorers caught sight of Sierra Leone's mountains and coastal shoreline in the mid-15th century, they found a land whose inhabitants were actively trading with people from Mali and other parts of Western Africa. Portuguese sailors Alvaro Fernandez and Pedro da Cintra were the first Europeans to visit the Sierra Leone peninsula and initiate trade with Western Europe. Da Cintra is credited with naming the area *Serra Lyoa*, or "Lion Mountains."

Soon, more ships bringing Portuguese and British merchants arrived at the country's well-protected harbor, the site of today's city of Freetown. Initially, they exchanged goods such as swords, kitchen utensils, and fabric for ivory and timber. Later, they also established the slave trade—the capture, sale, and transport of black Africans to other parts of the world.

Foreign merchants built trading posts in the region and negotiated agreements with the leaders of individual chiefdoms. Although Portugal's influence soon waned, other European countries, including Great Britain, France, Denmark, and the Netherlands, established trading networks in Africa.

By the late 17th century, the slave trade was flourishing all along the West African coast. However, at the same time a number of British people were beginning to voice opposition to the practice of slavery, and the movement to abolish it was growing.

During the 15th century Portuguese ships like these explored the Atlantic coast of Africa. In 1462 a Portuguese explorer named Pedro da Cintra landed in what is today Sierra Leone and gave the region its name.

COLONIZATION AND GOVERNANCE

The first step towards colonization of Sierra Leone was a result of *philanthropic* efforts by proponents of the antislavery movement in Great Britain. British abolitionists such as Granville Sharp, William Wilberforce, and Thomas Clarkson not only wanted to outlaw the slave trade but also believed that freed slaves belonged back in Africa. Through their efforts, freed African slaves from Britain and the newly formed United States of America, as well as displaced blacks from other places, such as Jamaica and Nova Scotia, were brought to a colony on the Sierra Leone peninsula.

The first settlers arrived in 1787. Despite bad weather, illness, and disease—as well as attacks on the ships bringing the freed slaves to their new home—the settlement took hold. Its inhabitants called their new home Freetown, and in 1808 it became a British *crown colony.*

Many of the former slaves who settled in Freetown were not originally from the Sierra Leone region. They had lived in other parts of Africa before being enslaved and transported to the Americas or Europe. These freed slaves had been away from Africa for a long time and no longer felt connected with their former ways of life, traditions, and culture. When they settled in Freetown, they brought with them various African customs and languages that had blended with those of the Americans, British, and other Europeans.

These new residents of Freetown came to be known as the Krio community. Most of them flourished economically, building up lucrative trade businesses all along the western coast of Africa. In time, the indigenous people of Sierra Leone would come to resent the wealth and prominence the Krio enjoyed as favored citizens of the British colony.

THE COLONY GROWS

During the 1800s Freetown prospered and grew. One of its strengths was its educational system, which was supported by the Society for Missions to Africa and the East (later called the Church Missionary Society, or CMS). The organization had been founded by abolitionists like William Wilberforce and Henry

Thornton to spread Christianity throughout West Africa. CMS established schools in the new British colony of Sierra Leone, including the Christian Institute, founded in 1814. The institute ultimately became a school to train teachers and clergymen. Later renamed Fourah Bay College, the school was affiliated in 1876 with Durham University, in Great Britain, thus becoming West Africa's first university.

As a crown colony, Freetown was administered by Great Britain. For many years the British appointed the governor and seven other officials who oversaw the colony, while the black inhabitants of Freetown had no say in its politics. However, over time the freed slaves gained a voice. Participation in their government began with the founding of the local private paper *The New Era*, in 1855. Later, in 1863, a special board called the Legislative Council was formed to advise the British rulers. Freetown's first elected representative was John Ezzidio, a Nigerian who had been rescued from a slave ship as a boy and sent to Freetown. However, the British government later changed its policy of allowing elections by the local people. Instead, the colonial government began to appoint its own representatives to the Legislative Council.

As Freetown prospered, the British began to expand their control in Sierra Leone further inland. To prevent the French from claiming the interior, Great Britain declared the region a British *protectorate* in 1896. The British government imposed taxes on the Krio, who continued to resent their lack of representation in the local government. Finally, in 1924, the residents of Sierra Leone were permitted to elect members to the Legislative Council.

WORLD WARS

Since their country was part of the British Commonwealth, Sierra Leonean soldiers served and fought under the British flag during the major global conflicts of the first half of the 20th century. During World War I (1914–1918), the Sierra Leone Battalion fought alongside the regiments of other African countries under British rule. With the aid of soldiers from Nigeria, Gambia, and the Gold Coast, army units from Sierra Leone defeated German colonial forces in the German-held territories of Togoland and Kamerun (today's Cameroon) between 1914 and 1916.

The onset of the Second World War in 1939 brought further growth to Sierra Leone. Freetown became an important Allied military base of operations for the British, with the natural harbor of Freetown offering excellent access in and out of the western coast of Africa. Sierra Leonean troops supported various British military campaigns, including the Southeast Asia effort in Burma, where more than 17,000 Sierra Leonean troops fought in 1945.

INDEPENDENCE

At the end of World War II, in 1945, the Allies were victorious, but the British had been drained economically and politically. Around this time, there was an increased movement among Sierra Leoneans for independence. A provisional constitution written in 1951 outlined the steps towards *decolonization*. It called for granting more governmental power to the people of Sierra Leone, although its terms favored the indigenous people living in the British protectorate over the Krios. Because their numbers were small, accounting for only a small percentage of the Sierra Leone population, the Krios (who lived mainly in the colony) were given little representation in the new government. Friction between the Krios of the colony and the indigenous people of the protectorate grew as both groups vied for majority rule and a say in the governance of their country.

Of the many people working for independence from Britain, none was more influential than Milton Margai. A medical doctor and political activist of Mende descent, Margai had been educated at Fourah Bay College, in Sierra Leone, and King's College, in London. He was active in the communities in the protectorate, where he divided his time between healing the sick and working in politics.

At the time the provisional constitution was written, Margai was the chairman of the Sierra Leone People's Party (SLPP). This political party had been established to advocate for the well being of all people of Sierra Leone, and to work to include them in the affairs of their country. In 1953, the British introduced a local ministerial system of government in Sierra Leone, and in 1954 Margai was appointed chief minister of the country. Over the next few years, he skillfully negotiated with the British government to put together a permanent constitution. Ultimately, Sierra Leone decided to accept a *parliamentary* system of governance within the British Commonwealth of Nations. (Remaining part of the Commonwealth granted Sierra Leone economic advantages when trading with other Commonwealth nations.)

Margai's greatest strength was his ability to work with all factions within Sierra Leone. When Great Britain officially declared Sierra Leone an

Sierra Leone's second prime minister (1964–67), Albert Margai headed an administration that was criticized for its widespread corruption.

independent country on April 27, 1961, Milton Margai became the nation's first prime minister. In efforts to make his government inclusive, he offered positions in his cabinet to opposition leaders, who included his brother Albert Margai.

One of Albert Margai's allies was Siaka Stevens, who in 1960 had formed an opposition party that eventually became known as the All People's Congress, or APC. A member of the Limba tribe, Stevens gained support in the more rural northern and western parts of Sierra Leone. In the 1962 elections he and his party mounted a challenge to Milton Margai and the SLPP. Although the APC won 16 of the 62 seats in the parliament, the SLPP retained control of the government and Margai remained prime minister.

A WAVE OF MILITARY COUPS

Margai lived for only two years after his election, during a time of relative stability in Sierra Leone. Upon his death in 1964, his brother Albert assumed the position of prime minister. While Albert Margai was focusing his attention on the growth and further development of the new nation, Siaka Stevens was picking up support throughout the country. Despite his *incumbency*, Margai lost to Stevens in the next elections, held in March 1967.

However, before Stevens could be sworn in, Brigadier David Lansana intervened and seized power in a military coup. A few days later, on March 23, junior officers in the military carried out another coup. They placed Lansana under arrest and suspended Sierra Leone's constitution. The political turmoil quickly led to another coup, on March 30, when Brigadier Juxon Smith assumed power. A year later, he was overthrown by a band of low-ranking soldiers in the army. They returned Siaka Stevens and his APC Party to power.

As prime minister, Stevens did not bring political stability to Sierra Leone. He filled all of his cabinet posts with APC members. Many ethnic groups resented their exclusion from participation in their government, and civil unrest swept the country.

After another coup attempt in 1971, the government adopted a new constitution and declared the country a republic. Stevens was appointed president until parliamentary elections could be held. In 1973 Stevens and the APC won overwhelmingly, and despite massive student protests, he was reelected in 1977. A year later he helped guide the passage of a constitutional referendum that made the APC Sierra Leone's only legal political party.

Siaka Stevens took over as prime minister in 1968, and became president in 1971. During his 17 years of rule he established a one-party dictatorship and amassed a personal fortune, while bankrupting the country.

CIVIL UNREST

Stevens assumed control over the nation's diamond industry, funneling its wealth into his bank accounts instead of into administrative budgets. As a result, the government could not fund its educational and civil services. The economy struggled as the number of uneducated and unemployed youth grew, and as professional workers fled the country. While Stevens and other corrupt officials enjoyed lavish lifestyles, most of the people of Sierra Leone lived in poverty.

Foday Sankoh formed the Revolutionary United Front (RUF) and led the insurrection against Sierra Leone's government that began in 1991. In May 2000 Sankoh was arrested. After being indicted for war crimes, he died in 2003 of natural causes.

Discontent with the government continued to grow among the young people of the country. One of those who decided to fight against the country's corruption and authoritarian leadership was Foday Sankoh, a former Sierra Leone army corporal. In the late 1980s, Sankoh traveled to Libya, where its radical leader, Muammar al-Gadhafi, was sponsoring military-type training programs in an attempt to ignite revolutions throughout West Africa.

While in Libya, Foday Sankoh met Charles Taylor, who was leading a rebellion in his own country of Liberia. Taylor, then a rebel warlord and later president of Liberia, became a chief financial backer and supporter of Sankoh's efforts to overthrow the government of Sierra Leone. Sankoh returned to his country in the early 1990s, and with allies Abu Kanu and Rashid Mansaray formed a new political party called the Revolutionary United Front (RUF). The rebels promised free health care and schooling to the poverty-stricken people of Sierra Leone, who initially supported them. The party managed to recruit many members who shared their goal of overthrowing the government.

By the time Sankoh returned to Sierra Leone, Siaka Stevens had retired from the presidency. After Stevens stepped down in 1985, his APC party had endorsed only one candidate to replace him: General Joseph Saidu Momoh.

The new president was aware of the corruption of his predecessors, and tried to distance himself from them. He even put together a cabinet composed of civilians, instead of military officials. Momoh was interested in promoting Sierra Leone as a country dedicated to ensuring human rights and democratic principles. He appointed a commission to review the country's one-party system and subsequently supported the passage of a new constitution in 1991 that provided for multiparty rule. Despite his efforts to improve the government, however, the president could not stop Sierra Leone from its descent into civil war.

CIVIL WAR

Armed and outfitted with weapons and military supplies provided by Liberian warlord Charles Taylor (who was paid with diamonds from the mines that the RUF controlled in eastern Sierra Leone), the RUF militia began fighting the government in March 1991. The rebels began a campaign of unspeakable terror and

A child soldier of the RUF. During Sierra Leone's civil war, children were commonly abducted from their homes and forced into combat. Child soldiers have had a difficult time assimilating back into society.

brutality against the very civilians they had once championed. Members of the RUF murdered, raped, and tortured anyone who resisted. Thousands of victims were mutilated with knives or had their limbs or hands amputated. As it cut a path of destruction throughout the country, the RUF abducted children as young as six years old and forced them to become soldiers or slaves.

With control of the diamond mine region and no restrictions on its movements, the RUF kept Sierra Leoneans in constant fear for their lives. The country was plunged into a series of economic and humanitarian crises as agricultural production came to a standstill; the mines closed; and scores of schools, health facilities, and administration buildings were destroyed. In efforts to escape the ruthless slaughter, hundreds of thousands of Sierra Leoneans fled their homes, many seeking refuge in neighboring countries.

To counter the attacks, Momoh doubled the size of the army. However, the government did not have the funds to arm or pay its soldiers. Then, in April 1992, Momoh was ousted from power in a military coup led by Captain Valentine Strasser. He immediately suspended the constitution and established a new party, called the National Provisional Ruling Council (NPRC). At first, Strasser tried to continue the fight against the RUF, but the military campaign proved unsuccessful. Two years after coming to power, he attempted to end the civil war by negotiating a cease-fire. Negotiations also failed, and the war raged on.

Strasser eventually agreed to return Sierra Leone to a civilian government and to hold presidential and legislative elections. Before the elections took place, however, he was ousted in another coup in January 1996 and sent into exile.

Elections were held a month later, and SLPP candidate Ahmad Tejan Kabbah won the presidency. Shortly after assuming power in March 1996, he successfully negotiated a truce with the rebels—the Abidjan Peace Accord, signed in November of 1996.

However, the agreement did not end the fighting. In May 1997, a new rebel group calling itself the Armed Forces Revolutionary Council (AFRC) overthrew Kabbah, who fled the country. Its leader, Johnny Paul Koroma, invited the RUF to join the AFRC in a joint military government. The horrific rampage of murder, looting, and rape continued.

THE INTERNATIONAL COMMUNITY INTERVENES

With Sierra Leoneans starving, their country in shambles, and the refugee crisis worsening, the international community stepped in. A peacekeeping force made up of troops from West African nations, known as ECOMOG (the Economic Community of West African States Monitoring Group), entered Sierra Leone. After months of fierce fighting, ECOMOG drove Koroma and the AFRC out of Freetown. In the spring of 1998, Kabbah was restored to his post as president.

However, the AFRC and the RUF still retained control over most of the country outside the capital city. In January 1999, the rebels mounted another bloody attack on Freetown. ECOMOG troops eventually drove them back out of the capital. That July, Sankoh and Kabbah signed a peace agreement that called for a new transitional unity government.

The peace agreement, known as the Lomé Peace Accord, was named for the city in Togo where negotiations took place. It granted the RUF four cabinet and four ministerial posts, and it established the RUF as a political party. Sankoh and his rebels were promised full amnesty for war crimes, while Kabbah was assured that the rebels would demobilize and turn in their weapons.

Within a few months, however, the peace agreement ran into trouble. In October 1999, the United Nations (an international organization that works to preserve world peace) replaced ECOMOG with a UN peace-keeping force. Known as the United Nations Mission in Sierra Leone, or UNAMSIL, the group was tasked with making the agreement between Kabbah's government and Sankoh's rebels work. However, in May 2000,

Villagers in Moyamba gather walk past a United Nations vehicle used by peacekeeping troops in their village. The United Nations sent more than 17,000 soldiers to end the fighting and disarm RUF combatants.

the peace agreement collapsed when the RUF took 500 UNAMSIL soldiers hostage.

Concerned about the safety of British citizens living in Sierra Leone, Great Britain immediately launched a military action, code-named Operation Palliser. In addition to supporting the UN peacekeeping force, the British troops helped secure the airports to allow foreign nationals to evacuate and UN supplies to be shipped in. During the six-week military action, British forces arrested Sankoh and some of his subordinates.

RECOVERY BEGINS

The war did not officially end for another two years. During that time UNAMSIL worked to bring about peace and to disarm the rebel militias throughout the country. Eventually, approximately 70,000 rebels—many of them child soldiers—would turn in their weapons and be reintegrated back into civil society. The UN force also assisted with national elections and in the rebuilding of government services and the police force.

The last phase of the disarmament was completed in January 2002. Sierra Leone held elections that spring, and Ahmad Tejan Kabbah was reelected to a five-year term. His SLPP party won 83 of the 122 legislative seats available, and although the RUF was permitted to have candidates on the ballot, not a single member was elected.

Sierra Leone's decade-long civil war devastated the nation. During the course of the war, more than 50,000 people died and thousands more were wounded or maimed. Approximately 2 million people (about half of the country's population at the time) were forced to flee their homes.

Alhaji Ahmad Tejan Kabbah served as president of Sierra Leone from 1996 to 1997, and again from 1998 to 2007. Under Sierra Leone's constitution, he is not eligible to serve in that position again because he has already been elected to two terms.

While the Sierra Leone government struggles to repair its country, war crimes trials have brought some of the worst figures to justice. RUF leader Foday Sankoh died in 2003, while under indictment for crimes against humanity. After fleeing to Liberia, AFRC leader Johnny Paul Koroma was reportedly killed the same year. Former Liberian president Charles Taylor, who had been ousted from power after a bloody civil war in Liberia, was captured in March 2006. Indicted in 2003 for war crimes by the Special Court for Sierra Leone, Taylor had successfully avoided prosecution for three years. His trial, which opened in June of 2007, lasted until April 2012. Taylor was found guilty of all 11 charges levied by the Special Court for Sierra Leone, including terror, murder and rape

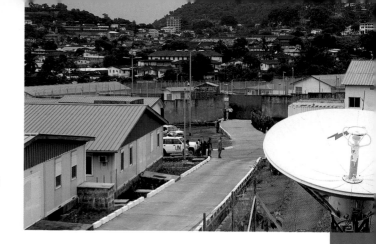

(Opposite) Sierra Leone's president Ernest Bai Koroma (left) greets UN Secretary Ban Ki-moon at UN headquarters in New York. The United Nations has remained involved in Sierra Leone since the late 1990s. (Right) The Sierra Leone Special Court holds war crime trials in this facility in Freetown.

3 A More Secure Government

AFTER HAVING GONE THROUGH so much suffering and strife during their country's civil war, the people of Sierra Leone have begun the slow process of rebuilding their country. The National Pledge of Sierra Leone reflects the deep commitment felt by its citizens. It reads:

> I pledge my love and loyalty to my country Sierra Leone;
> I vow to serve her faithfully at all times;
> I promise to defend her honour and good name;
> Always work for her unity, peace, freedom and prosperity
> And put her interest above all else.
> So help me God.

Sierra Leone's constitution, approved in 1991, established the country as an independent republic. In this form of democracy, the power to govern belongs to representatives chosen by the general population in open, free elections. Sierra Leone has a multiparty system of government, which means that representatives can be elected from a variety of political parties.

When it gained independence from Britain in 1961, Sierra Leone had just one political party. Today, there are almost two dozen parties, including the Sierra Leone People's Party, All People's Congress, People's Democratic Party, and the People's Movement for Democratic Change. All have the same rights and opportunities to put up candidates for election. Under the 1991 constitution, elections for the president and the legislature take place every five years. All Sierra Leone citizens are permitted to take part in the election process and are eligible to vote upon reaching the age of 18.

Sierra Leone is divided into four administrative regions: the Northern, Southern, and Eastern Provinces and the Western Area. Representatives from each of these areas play a part in the country's government, which consists of three separate branches: executive, legislative, and judicial.

THE EXECUTIVE BRANCH

The president heads the executive branch of the government. His responsibilities are described in Chapter V of Sierra Leone's constitution: "The President shall be the Fountain of Honour and Justice and the symbol of national unity and *sovereignty*. The President shall be the guardian of the Constitution and the guarantor of national independence and territorial integrity, and shall ensure respect for treaties and international agreements."

The president of Sierra Leone holds three important titles—chief of state, head of the government, and minister of defense. To qualify to run for the presidency, a person must be a citizen of Sierra Leone, belong to a political party, and be at least 40 years old. The president may serve only two five-year terms, although they need not be consecutive. An elected vice president assists the president with his duties.

The executive branch also includes a cabinet, whose members are appointed by the president. In Sierra Leone, these government officials are referred to as ministers or deputy ministers. The cabinet of President Ernest Bai Koroma, who was elected to a five-year term in the 2007 election, is comprised of 18 ministers who help the president and vice president in administering the functions of the government. Each ministry covers a specific area of the government, such as finance, health, transportation, communication, education, or trade. There are also three ministers of state, or regional ministers, who represent the Eastern, Northern, and Southern Provinces.

THE LEGISLATIVE BRANCH

The legislative branch of Sierra Leone's government is known as the parliament. Also referred to as the House of Representatives, it is *unicameral* (consisting of just one legislative chamber). The job of the parliament is to make the laws to ensure the peace, security, and proper governance of Sierra Leone.

There are 124 members of parliament. Twelve seats are reserved for paramount chiefs (the heads of chiefdoms; each representing one of the 12 districts of Sierra Leone's provinces). The political party controlling the remaining 112 seats is determined by the percentage of votes the party receives during elections. For example, in 2007, the All People's Congress received 40.7 percent of the vote, thereby winning 59 seats. The SLPP won

39.5 percent of the votes, and won 43 seats, while the PMDC won 15.3 percent, gaining 10 seats.

The parliament conducts all legislative business in the Parliament Building at Tower Hill, Freetown. A memorial statue of Milton Margai stands in front of the Parliament Building, as a tribute to Sierra Leone's first elected prime minister.

THE JUDICIAL SYSTEM

Oversight of all civil and criminal matters, including those related to constitutional issues, falls under the jurisdiction of the judiciary branch of the Sierra Leone government. The judiciary is made up of the lower courts (district and local courts) and higher courts (the Supreme Court, the Court of Appeal, and a High Court). Cases are heard first in the lower courts and upon appeal move up to higher courts. Judges are appointed by the president and approved by the House.

Magistrates—civil officers who are members of the judiciary with the authority to enforce law—operate in many of Sierra Leone's 12 districts. Appeals of decisions made by magistrate courts are heard by the High Court.

There are also many local courts throughout the 148 chiefdoms in Sierra Leone. Elected native leaders oversee these courts and handle civil disputes according to traditional and cultural customs and practices.

In 2000, the government of Sierra Leone requested that the United Nations help it establish a joint judicial body to prosecute those responsible for the atrocities committed during the country's civil war. The resulting Special Court, located in the capital city of Freetown, became operational in

2003. It works to bring to justice those who participated in war crimes, crimes against humanity, and other violations of international law.

TRUTH AND RECONCILIATION

The United Nations also supported the establishment of the Sierra Leone Truth and Reconciliation Commission (TRC), a forum whose establishment was required by the 1999 Lomé Peace Accord. The purpose of the Commission was to promote the healing of wounds to the country's society that were caused by the decade-long conflict.

The TRC began public hearings in April 2003. In documenting abuses, the Commission collected more than 7,700 statements from victims of atrocities. The hearings gave war crime victims the opportunity to face their attackers. However, the TRC did not mete out punishments. Instead, it served to provide a forum for both abuser and victim to voice their experiences and try to achieve reconciliation.

The purpose of the Truth and Reconciliation Commission was also to determine how to prevent similar wartime atrocities from occurring again. Among the recommendations made by the TRC in its final report, published in October 2004, were suggestions to strengthen the judiciary and rule of law, and to establish policies to prevent future government corruption.

(Opposite) Sierra Leone's poor infra-structure hampers economic development. During the rainy season unpaved roads become muddy bogs, making it difficult to transport goods. (Right) Cassava is a staple of the Sierra Leonean diet. It grows well in harsh soil and yields more calories per acre than almost any other food crop.

4 Challenges for the Economy

SIERRA LEONE IS A COUNTRY BLESSED with abundant mineral, agricultural, and oceanic resources. In addition, it features beautiful countryside and beaches that have the potential to attract many tourism dollars. But despite having significant resources that normally would boost a country's economy and provide jobs, Sierra Leone still suffers the effects of its devastating civil war. Recovery has been slow.

According to the United Nations Human Development Report, which annually ranks the quality of life in countries (based on indicators such as income, life expectancy, and literacy), Sierra Leone consistenly ranks at the bottom. Seventy percent of the population earns about one dollar a day. An almost equal percentage is *illiterate*. Many men, women, and children often go hungry and are undernourished.

THE ECONOMY OF SIERRA LEONE

Gross domestic product (GDP*):
$4.72 billion (2010 est.)

Inflation: 11.7% (2007 est.)

Natural resources: diamonds, rutile, bauxite, iron, gold, chromite

Agriculture (49% of GDP): rice, coffee, cocoa, palm kernels, palm oil, peanuts, poultry, cattle, sheep, pigs, fish (2005)

Industry (31% of GDP): diamond mining, small-scale manufacturing (beverages, textiles, cigarettes, footwear), petroleum refining, small commercial ship repair (2005)

Services (21% of GDP): government, other (2005)

Foreign trade:
Exports—$216 million: diamonds, rutile, cocoa, coffee, fish (2006)
Imports—$560 million: foodstuffs, machinery and equipment, fuels and lubricants, chemicals (2006)

Economic growth rate: 5% (2010 est.)

Currency exchange rate: U.S. $1 = 4,319 leones (2011)

*GDP is the total value of goods and services produced in a country annually.
All figures are 2010 estimates unless otherwise indicated.
Source: CIA World Factbook, 2011.

Several factors have hindered Sierra Leone's economic recovery. They include the country's inadequate *infrastructure*, its high rate of unemployment, and its dependence on *subsistence farming*.

The transportation infrastructure of Sierra Leone was inadequate even before the civil war. Today, Sierra Leone needs to build, repair, and make improvements to its roads, railroads, bridges, ports, and airports in order to efficiently move goods to and from markets. In addition, the government needs to provide electricity, public transportation, water supplies, mail services, health care, and schools for its people.

Unemployment, particularly among Sierra Leone's youth and ex-rebels, threatens future peace, as well as economic development. Most young people in the country lack an education and training. Those living in poverty may again engage in conflict if they come to believe their government is mismanaging the country's natural resources, particularly its diamonds.

Most farmed land in Sierra Leone produces only the bare minimum of what farmers and their families need to survive. If more farmers could increase their yields and move beyond subsistence farming, they could not only earn more revenue but also prevent food shortages.

The *gross domestic product* (GDP, the total value of goods and services that a nation produces) in Sierra Leone, which has a population of 6 million, was estimated at around $4.72 billion in 2010. By comparison, Puerto Rico, a territory with a population of just under 4 million, had a GDP of an estimated $65 billion in 2010. With its many natural resources, Sierra Leone should have had a much higher GDP.

However, the country's economy has shown some improvement. Its estimated GDP growth rate in 2010 was about 5 percent, while Puerto Rico's GDP shrunk by almost 6 percent.

AGRICULTURE

The agricultural industry employs between 60 and 70 percent of the workforce and contributes almost half (49 percent) of Sierra Leone's total GDP. Sierra Leone's most important agricultural food crops are rice, cassava, corn, millet, and peanuts. Rice is planted in *upland systems* (mountainous regions), particularly in the country's Northern Province.

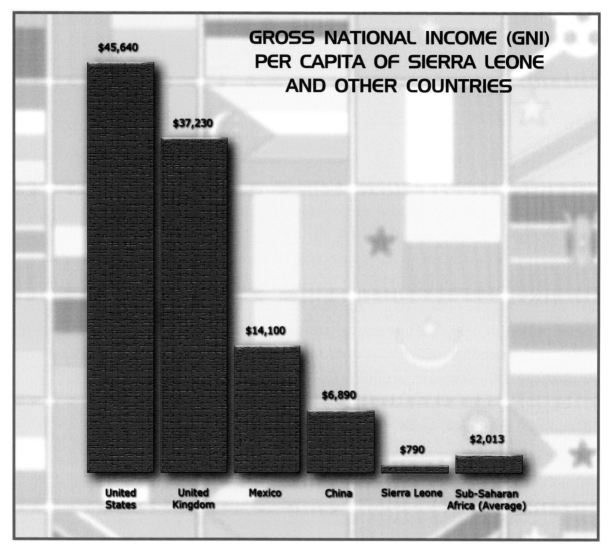

GROSS NATIONAL INCOME (GNI) PER CAPITA OF SIERRA LEONE AND OTHER COUNTRIES

$45,640 — United States
$37,230 — United Kingdom
$14,100 — Mexico
$6,890 — China
$790 — Sierra Leone
$2,013 — Sub-Saharan Africa (Average)

Gross national income per capita is the total value of all goods and services produced domestically in a year, supplemented by income received from abroad, divided by midyear population. The above figures take into account fluctuations in currency exchange rates and differences in inflation rates across global economies, so that an international dollar has the same purchasing power as a U.S. dollar has in the United States. Source: World Bank, 2011.

The most important crop exports include cocoa, coffee, palm kernels, and palm oil. Coffee and cocoa are grown on plantations in forested areas in the Eastern Province, near the cities of Kenema and Kailahun. Other agricultural exports include poultry, cattle, sheep, and pigs, which are raised on farms located throughout the country. Sierra Leone's fishing industry, located along the western coast and around offshore islands, provides another important source of export revenue.

MINING INDUSTRY

Mining is one of Sierra Leone's most important industries. The country has an abundance of valuable minerals, including gold, iron, diamonds, bauxite (used to make aluminum), and rutile (a major ore of titanium). One of the world's largest deposits of rutile is located in the Southern Province, in the coastal region.

In 2005, revenues from diamond exports reached $140 million—an increase of about 70 percent since the government regained control of diamond fields following the civil war. Sierra Leone has developed diamond reserves in almost one fourth of its total land area, with the highest concentrations in southeastern part of the country, in the Kenema, Kono, and Bo Districts.

Although most of the diamond fields in the country are now fully operating, many of the mines producing bauxite and rutile that shut down during the civil war have not reopened. Before the civil war, Sierra Leone was the world's third-largest producer of rutile, but as was the case with most of Sierra Leone's industries, the war ravaged the mining industry. Bauxite and

Mineral-rich Sierra Leone is a major producer of diamonds, which today account for one half of the country's exports.

rutile mines had been major employers and primary sources of revenue for the government, providing 75 percent of the country's exports. Recent foreign investments in some mines have financed their repair and reopening.

EFFORTS TO DEVELOP TOURISM

The Ministry of Tourism and Cultural Affairs was created in 1973 to develop programs that would promote economic development in Sierra Leone. Initially many visitors came to the country, because of its scenic beaches and resort communities. However, any potential for a strong tourism economy was devastated by the country's civil war. Images and reports of violence taking place in Sierra Leone during the 1980s and early 1990s effectively shut down the tourist industry.

Since the end of the war, and with the restoration of peace and stability, the government has renewed its efforts to boost the economy by attracting visitors to its beaches and nature preserves. Funds have been set aside to restore historic structures and to promote the development of restaurants, hotels, and other service facilities.

Another vital component to a strong tourist industry is an adequate transportation infrastructure. Among the projects to improve access in and out of the nation are improvements being made to international airports in Freetown and on Sherbro Island. By rebuilding its roads, as well as its communities destroyed by war, the government of Sierra Leone hopes to make the country appealing both to investors in the hospitality industry and to foreigners who are planning their next vacation.

The vibrant culture of Sierra Leone reflects a blending of many influences. (Right) The early inhabitants of Freetown were freed slaves who came from many different parts of Africa. (Opposite) The Refugee All Stars are displaced Sierra Leoneans who formed a band while living in a Guinea refugee camp. They play a mixture of West African goombay, reggae, and hip-hop.

5 The People of Sierra Leone

IN SIERRA LEONE, there are many diverse ethnic groups, each with distinct backgrounds, music, foods, dance, crafts, and attire. The present-day population of the country includes about 20 different African ethnic groups, as well as people from other lands.

THE MENDE

Comprising about one third of the total population, the Mende (also called the Mandingo) live in the southern region of Sierra Leone. Their language is closely related to the Mandé language, which is spoken by many ethnic groups in West Africa. The Mende are believed to be descended from the Mandé people, who migrated from the Sudan between the 2nd and 16th centuries.

The Mende have a rich artistic heritage, and place great value on music

THE PEOPLE OF SIERRA LEONE

Population: 5,363,669 (July 2011 est.)

Ethnic groups: Temne 35%, Mende 31%, Limba 8%, Kono 5%, Krio 2%, Mandingo 2%, Loko 2%, other 15% (includes refugees from Liberia's recent civil war, and small numbers of Europeans, Lebanese, Pakistanis, and Indians) (2008 census)

Age structure:
0–14 years: 41.8%
15–64 years: 54.5%
65 years and over: 3.7%

Birth rate: 38.46 births/1,000 population

Infant mortality rate: 73.38 deaths/1,000 live births

Death rate: 11.73 deaths/ 1,000 population

Population growth rate: 2.25%

Life expectancy at birth:
total population: 56.13 years
male: 53.69 year
female: 58.65 years

Total fertility rate: 4.94 children born/woman

Religions: Muslim 60%, indigenous beliefs 30%, Christian 10%

Languages: English (official, regular use limited to literate minority), Mende (principal language in the south), Temne (principal language in the north), Krio (English-based Creole)

Literacy: 35.1% (2004 est.)

All figures are 2011 estimates unless otherwise indicated.
Source: Adapted from CIA World Factbook, 2011.

and dance. Much of their art has a direct association to health and healing rituals, which typically incorporate the use of elaborately carved wooden masks. One kind of mask, known as the Bondu helmet, is the only one known to be worn exclusively by women.

Like other traditional ethnic groups of Africa, the Mende live in walled villages and form their own political divisions, called chiefdoms, which are headed by a paramount chief. Most engage in subsistence farming, growing rice, yams, and cassava. The Mende people who live near the waters of the Atlantic Ocean usually work in the fishing industry.

The Mende have traditionally been active in government politics, and have been known to participate in demonstrations to express their displeasure with the government. Most are major supporters of the Sierra Leone People's Party. The first president of Sierra Leone, Milton Margai, was a Mende.

THE TEMNE

Like the Mende, the Temne make up about 30 percent of the country's total population. They are also one of the oldest ethnic groups of Sierra Leone. Historians believe that they came from present-day Guinea in the 1400s. They were most likely the tribe that the Portuguese explorers encountered in the Northern Province when they first visited the West African coast in the 15th century.

The early Temne people settled along the coast between two of the country's important rivers, the Little Scarcies and the Sewa. Today, the group makes up the majority of the population in the Northern Province districts of Kambia and Port Loko.

There has been ongoing hostility between the Temne and Mende ethnic groups. However, the Temne have much in common with their southern counterparts: Like the Mende, the Temne are also farming people, growing crops like rice, peanuts, and cassava. Villagers living near the rivers typically fish for a living. Temne communities are divided into chiefdoms led by paramount chiefs. And the Temne consider music and dance as part of their way of life. For example, the Temne Rabai dance, which takes place once a year, is part of the culture's coming-of-age celebration.

THE KRIO COMMUNITY

Even though current estimates suggest that the Krio community makes up only about 2 percent of Sierra Leone's population, this group holds a very important place in the history and development of the country. Because the Krio are descendants of freed African slaves who originally settled Freetown, they were more inclined than the indigenous people of Sierra Leone to adopt European customs and practices. The Krio accepted Christian—not Islamic—beliefs and practices. They took English names, adopted European customs, and developed a unique language. Although the Krio language is English-based, the pronunciation, spelling, and sentence structure are heavily influenced by a mixture of African languages, particularly Yoruba.

Many Krio established significant trade businesses, often achieving status on par with that of white Europeans living in the colony. Krio children were educated at Fourah Bay College and took jobs within the government, often holding administrative and other well-paying positions within the colony. However, after the British government expanded its control farther inland and made the interior of Sierra Leone a protectorate in 1896, the status of the Krio diminished. Europeans and others from outside the country eventually took many of the more lucrative jobs in the medical sector and the military.

LIBERIAN REFUGEES

A significant part of Sierra Leone's population is Liberian. A brutal civil war in their country, from 1989 to 1996 and then again from 1999 to 2003, forced many citizens of Liberia to flee their homes. The two civil wars caused the deaths of more than 250,000 people. Another million became refugees; more than 70,000 of them fled to Sierra Leone.

Struggling to recover from its own civil war, to rebuild, and to feed its own population, the government of Sierra Leone has had to face a critical situation in addressing the needs of the large population of Liberian refugees. Some have been *repatriated* with the help of various UN agencies and other relief organizations.

EDUCATION CHALLENGES

After Freetown became a British crown colony in 1808, education became an integral part of the new colony's development. With the establishment of Fourah Bay College, Sierra Leone became one of the few countries in West Africa offering advanced educational opportunities. However, at around 65 percent, illiteracy rates are high in Sierra Leone today. Only about 40 percent of school-aged children attend some type of educational institution. Few have a school building in which to learn, because so many were destroyed or badly damaged during the war. Even in places where school buildings still stand, many children cannot

Muslim girls wear school uniforms in Freetown.

Players from the Single Leg Amputee Sports Club Sierra Leone (SLASC) face off in a match in Freetown. Founded in 2001, the SLASC provides trauma recovery for amputee victims of the long civil war.

attend because they need to work in order to earn money to help their starving families.

THE ARTS AND RECREATION

The ethnic diversity in Sierra Leone is reflected in the country's rich variety of cultural activities, which range from literature, to music and dance, to sports.

Several writers have earned international recognition for their works. Renowned authors include short-story writer Adelaide Casely-Hayford, novelist Dr. R. Sarif Easmon, and poet Syl Cheney-Coker.

Music and dance are an integral part of every Sierra Leonean's life. Music accompanies many important milestones, including births, deaths, and marriages. The drum is the heart of the sound for many dances. Another traditional instrument is the *balangi* (a type of xylophone).

Sierra Leone has also developed its own unique form of popular music, called *maringa*, which features the guitar. The instrument was introduced to Sierra Leone by the Portuguese.

One way that Sierra Leone shares its dance traditions with the rest of the world is through its national dance troupe. Made up of people from various ethnic groups, the Sierra Leone National Dance Troupe has been performing at venues around the world since the 1960s. Supported by the Ministry of Tourism and Cultural Affairs since the 1970s, the group showcases traditional dances, songs, and music that date to Sierra Leone's beginnings.

Recognizing that sports can entertain and connect its citizens, the Sierra Leone government provides recreation programs and activities through its Ministry of Youth and Sports. A favorite sport in the country is soccer, which many Sierra Leoneans enjoy both playing and watching. The country's national team, the Leone Stars, has often competed against the neighboring countries of Guinea, Liberia, and The Gambia.

(Opposite) With a population of about 1 million, Freetown is Sierra Leone's largest city. It is the nation's financial and cultural center. (Right) Graffiti is scrawled on a wall near an abandoned factory in Bo. The civil war had a devastating effect on Sierra Leone's communities.

6 From Harbor Port to Diamond Mines

MOST OF SIERRA LEONE'S CITIES and towns are sparsely populated. The greatest population density is in the Western Area, which includes the capital city of Freetown. Sierra Leone's other prominent cities include Bo, Kenema, Koidu-Sefadu, and Makeni.

FREETOWN

Lying on the Freetown peninsula along the coast of the Atlantic Ocean, Freetown is the site where Sierra Leone's modern history began. Founded in 1787, the town has grown to become the largest city in the country, with an estimated population of approximately 1 million. Freetown's natural harbor, known as the Queen Elizabeth II Quay, handles most of Sierra Leone's export goods. Among Freetown's many industries are cigarette manufacturing, rice milling, diamond cutting, petroleum refining, and fish packing.

Some significant buildings in Freetown include the Sierra Leone Museum, St. George's Cathedral (completed in 1828), and the Old Fourah Bay College. A famous landmark that sits in the center of town is a giant cotton tree that dates to when the first settlers arrived. Early residents prayed at the foot of the massive tree, which today is considered a symbol of peace and prosperity for Sierra Leone. Its likeness is incorporated into the Freetown City Council Coat of Arms.

BO

The former capital of the Protectorate of Sierra Leone (1930–1961), Bo is located in the Southern Province. With an estimated population of 215,000 people, it is Sierra Leone's second-largest city. Inhabited mostly by members of the Mende ethnic group, Bo is an important trading center for palm kernels and diamonds.

Because Bo is also the primary transportation, commercial, and educational hub for the interior of the country, aid relief organizations and charities are often based there. Many of them, such as SOS Children's Village, offer services specifically for young people, who make up a large percentage of Bo's population. Many of these youth are former soldier combatants so aid organizations in Bo have focused on programs that provide educational opportunities, jobs, and activities that teach tolerance and peace. One of the most popular events is the three-day Bo Peace Carnival, held each year in the spring.

KENEMA

Kenema, the third-largest city in Sierra Leone and the capital of the Eastern Province, is found in the southeastern part of the country. According to recent estimates, Kenema has a population of 170,000 residents. The city's early years of economic development were boosted by the railway that linked Freetown to Kenema, and supported the local logging and carpentry industries.

The discovery of diamond mines in the area in 1931 drastically changed the economy of Kenema and the surrounding region. However, the diamond mining industry did little to help Sierra Leone's economy, as the valuable gems were often used to bribe government leaders and encourage other forms of corruption. During the civil war, rebels used diamonds from the region to finance their operations.

People crowd the street in Kenema, Sierra Leone's diamond-trading capital.

Since the end of the war, the national government, with assistance from the United Nations, has taken steps to try to limit the illegal sale and exportation of diamonds out of Sierra Leone. It is hoped that such regulation would stop future trade in "blood diamonds"—the term used to describe diamonds that are sold to fund rebellions against established governments.

Civil unrest in the neighboring country of Liberia during the early 2000s flooded the city of Kenema and other southeastern towns of Sierra Leone with large numbers of refugees fleeing fighting and forced recruitment. Today, more than 60,000 Liberian refugees live in eight camps located in the Kenema and Bo Districts.

KOIDU-SEFADU

In the Kono District of the Eastern Province is Koidu-Sefadu, the fourth-largest city in Sierra Leone. Its name is often shortened to Koidu or Sefadu. Recent estimates calculate a population of 91,000.

At one time Koidu-Sefadu was the second-largest city in Sierra Leone. But ferocious fighting during the civil war took its toll on the area. Because it is located in a diamond-rich region, the city was frequently the site of battles between rebel and government forces struggling for control of the area's rich resources.

Today, with the help of aid workers, the Koidu Government Hospital has been rebuilt. Aid organizations, such as the UN Refugee Agency and the United Nations High Commissioner for Refugees (UNHCR), have assisted in drilling wells and rebuilding schools, clinics, and health centers.

MAKENI

Located slightly northeast of Freetown, Makeni is Sierra Leone's fifth-largest city. With an estimated population of 102,000, Makeni is the capital city of the Northern Province.

During the civil war Makeni served as the base of the Revolutionary United Front. Much fighting took place in and around the city, and most of the structures in Makeni were severely damaged or burned to the ground. Once a thriving market town, Makeni lay in ruins at the end of the war. However, many of Makeni's residents are now returning as rebuilding takes place.

Although very few of Sierra Leone's major cities were left untouched by the country's civil war, many are being helped by the international community, relief organizations, and charities. They are working with Sierra Leoneans to rebuild a country with much hope and promise for a better future.

A CALENDAR OF SIERRA LEONEAN FESTIVALS

January

On January 1, people usher in the **New Year's Day** with parties that begin the night before.

April

April 27 is **Independence Day**. The date is traditionally marked by parades and other celebrations held around the country. In central Freetown, the **Lantern Parade** attracts as many as 100,000 people.

December

December 25 is **Christmas Day**. On this day Christians celebrate the birth of Jesus and exchange gifts. The day often celebrated in Sierra Leone with masquerade performances, parades, and parties.

A British tradition that falls on December 26 is **Boxing Day**. Many people celebrate the day with music, dancing, and picnics.

Religious Observances

Sierra Leone's Muslims and Christians observe several holy days related to their religions. Some of these fall on specific days of each year (for example, **Christmas** (which celebrates the birth of Jesus Christ) is observed on December 25. Many other major celebrations occur according to the lunar calendar, in which the months correspond to the phases of the moon. A lunar month is shorter than a typical month of the Western calendar. Therefore, the festival dates vary from year to year. Other celebrations are observed seasonally.

A very important month of the Muslim lunar calendar is the ninth month, **Ramadan**. This is a time of sacrifice for devout Muslims. During Ramadan, Muslims are not supposed to eat or drink between sunup and sundown. They are also supposed to restrict their activities during these hours to necessary duties, such a going to work. After the sun has set completely, Muslims make a special prayer before eating a small meal. Muslims mark the end of Ramadan with a celebration called **Eid al-Fitr**, or "breaking of the fast." During this time families get together and exchange gifts.

Eid al-Adha (Feast of the Sacrifice) takes place in the last month of the Muslim calendar during the **hajj** period, when Muslims make a pilgrimage to Mecca. The holiday honors the prophet

A CALENDAR OF SIERRA LEONEAN FESTIVALS

Abraham, who was willing to sacrifice his own son to Allah (God). In the story, God provided a sheep to be sacrificed instead. According to tradition, Muslim families slaughter and eat a sheep on this day. On Eid al-Adha, families traditionally eat a portion of the feast and donate the rest to the poor.

Another holy day is **Mawlid al-Nabiy**, or the birth of the Prophet. Muslims celebrate this day with prayer and often a procession to the local mosque. Families gather for feasts, which often feature the foods said to have been favored by Mohammed: dates, grapes, almonds, and honey. The holiday falls on the 12th day of the third month of the Islamic calendar, known as Rabi'-ul-Awwal.

The major Christian festivals that fall according to the lunar calendar involve the suffering and death of Jesus Christ. **Ash Wednesday** marks the start of a period of self-sacrifice called **Lent**, which lasts for 40 days. The final days of Lent are known as **Holy Week**. During this time a number of important days are observed, including **Palm Sunday**, which commemorates Jesus' arrival in Jerusalem; **Holy Thursday**, which marks the night of the last Supper; **Good Friday**, the day of Jesus' death on the cross; and **Easter Monday**, which marks his resurrection. (In Western countries, **Easter** is typically celebrated on the day before.)

In Sierra Leone, the Muslim holy days of **Eid al-Adha**, **Eid al-Fitr**, and **Mawlid al-Nabiy** are celebrated as national holidays. The Christian holy days of **Christmas**, **Good Friday**, and **Easter Monday** are also national holidays in the country.

RECIPES

West African Groundnut Stew

2 sweet potatoes
2 Tbsp. vegetable oil
3 garlic cloves, minced
3 Tbsp. grated ginger
2 Tbsp. coriander
1/2 tsp. cayenne
1 medium onion, chopped
2 medium tomatoes, chopped
4 cups eggplant, chopped
1 cups zucchini, chopped
2 green peppers, chopped
2 cups tomato juice
1/2 cup peanut butter

Directions:
1. Boil potatoes until just tender. Set aside.
2. Sauté garlic and ginger with rest of the spices for one minute. Add onion and sauté a few minutes longer. Add tomatoes, eggplant, and a bit of water. Simmer for 10 minutes.
3. Add zucchini and peppers and simmer another 20 minutes.
4. Drain potatoes and mash (leaving lumps), and then add to stew along with juice and peanut butter. Stir well. Simmer 5 to 10 minutes. Serve on rice or millet and garnish with pineapple or banana slices.

Adapted from http://www.astray.com/recipes

Benne Cakes (Sesame Cookies)

3/4 cup butter, softened
1 1/2 cup brown sugar
2 eggs, beaten
1 1/4 cup all-purpose flour
1/2 cup sesame seeds, toasted
1 tsp. vanilla extract
1/4 tsp. baking power

Directions:
1. Cream butter and sugar together and mix with other ingredients, in the order as listed.
2. Using a teaspoon, drop spoonfuls of dough on cookie sheet. Bake at 325° F for 30 minutes.

Adapted from www.nancyskitchen.com

Spinach Plasas

2 packages frozen chopped spinach
1/2 lb. smoked fish, flaked
1 large onion, chopped
1/4 cup groundnut paste (peanut butter)
3 cups water
1 1/2 cups palm oil
2 hot peppers or 1 tsp. cayenne pepper
1 pound meat, stewing or chuck roast

Directions:

1. Cut up meat. Put in saucepan with two cups of water, salt, onion, and pepper. Bring to boil and add palm oil. Partially cover saucepan with lid and continue cooking for 1-1/2 hours over medium heat.
2. Add spinach (previously thawed and drained), flaked fish and groundnut paste mixed with water. Stir, cover, and simmer for 10 minutes.
3. Serve with steamed rice.

Adapted from http://www.sierra-leone.org/recipes.html

GLOSSARY

abolitionist—person who works to end slavery.

ancestral—pertaining to an ancestor, who is someone from whom one is descended.

crown colony—colony whose legislature and administration is under control of the British government, or Crown.

decolonization—act of freeing a country from colonial status.

gross domestic product—the market value of all the goods and services produced in a country.

harmattan—a strong, dust-laden wind that blows off the Sahara into West Africa.

illiterate—unable to read or write.

incumbent—an official who is currently in office.

indigenous—originating from or native to a particular region.

infrastructure—the basic facilities and services of day-to-day economic activity.

Krio—language of the residents of Freetown, Sierra Leone; also the name for the mixed ethnic group descended from former slaves.

parliament—government based on a legislative assembly.

philanthropic—intended to help others for the common good.

plateau—a relatively flat, level surface of land, generally raised above an adjoining piece of land.

protectorate—a territory that is under the control, or "protection," of another government.

rainforest—wooded area with an annual rainfall of 100 inches (254 cm) or more.

referendum—a proposal submitted for acceptance or rejection in a vote by the entire country.

repatriate—to return to one's country of origin.

savanna—a tropical or subtropical grassland.

sovereignty—the authority of a state to govern free from external control.

subsistence farming—producing only enough food to feed a person and his or her family members.

unicameral—a legislative body consisting of only one chamber.

upland—elevated or mountainous land.

PROJECT AND REPORT IDEAS

Highest Mountains in West Africa

Research information on the tallest mountain peaks in the countries of West Africa (Benin, Gambia, Ghana, Guinea, the Ivory Coast, Mali, Nigeria, Togo, Senegal, and Sierra Leone). Make a list of each country's tallest mountain and height, and then illustrate your findings on graph paper. Use one block to represent 100 feet in height, showing West Africa's tallest mountains in order from lowest to highest. Use different colors for each peak, and label each mountain with its name and country.

Answer the following:

- Which country in West Africa has the tallest mountain? The shortest?
- What is the difference in feet from the tallest to the shortest?

Animals of Sierra Leone

Sierra Leone has an abundance of wildlife. Select two animals to research (such as the pygmy hippopotamus and elephant) and write a one-page report on each. Report on the animal's habitat, preferred climate (such as the colder mountains or warmer savanna), food, other places in the world where it can be found, how it raises its young, and so on. Is this animal endangered? If so, why?

Photocopy a map of the world. Color in each country where your researched animals live, using a different color for each animal. Are the animals you chose found in many places in the world? Are the climates the same or different?

Gullah Language

The Krio of Sierra Leone are believed to be related to the Gullah people who live in South Carolina and speak a language that is similar to Krio. Make a list of 20 words in English and use the Internet to look up the equivalent word in Gullah. Write the Gullah word down next to its English counterpart. Do you see any similarities in the two languages? Are certain letters of the alphabet used more than others in Gullah words? Can you understand Gullah if you read it out loud? Find some phrases to present to the class.

Sierra Leone Notable People

Write a one-page biography about one of the following people in Sierra Leone's history:

John Akar	McCormack Easmon
Solomon Ekuma Dominic Berewa	Ahmad Tejan Kabbah
Sylvia Olayinka Blyden	Milton Margai
Emmerson Bockarie	Foday Sankoh
Pedro da Cintra	Siaka Probyn Stevens

Learn More About Africa

Great Britain was not the only European country involved in the colonization of African nations. Research at least 10 African countries to determine which European country colonized each one, and the date it officially came under control of that foreign government. Then answer the following questions:

- Which African country was colonized first?
- Which African nation was the last to be colonized?
- How long was the country under colonial rule?
- Which country achieved independence first?
- Which country was the last to achieve independence?

CHRONOLOGY

1787: British abolitionists and philanthropists establish Freetown as a settlement for former slaves.

1808: The Freetown settlement becomes a British crown colony.

1896: Britain declares a protectorate over the interior, establishing the Colony and Protectorate of Sierra Leone.

1954: Milton Margai, head of the Sierra Leone People's Party, is appointed chief minister.

1961: Sierra Leone gains independence, and Milton Margai becomes the first prime minister.

1967: In a military coup Siaka Stevens's newly elected government is overthrown.

1968: Stevens returns to power following another military coup.

1971: Sierra Leone is declared a republic; Stevens becomes president.

1978: Passage of a constitutional referendum makes Sierra Leone a one-party state; the All People's Congress becomes the sole legal party.

1985: General Joseph Saidu Momoh assumes the presidency following Stevens's retirement.

1991: Civil war breaks out in Sierra Leone when Foday Sankoh and the Revolutionary United Front (RUF) take control of towns along the border with Liberia. In September, a new constitution is adopted that allows for a multiparty system.

1992: Captain Valentine Strasser leads a successful military coup to oust Momoh.

1996: In January, Strasser is overthrown in a military coup, and the following month Ahmad Tejan Kabbah is elected president. Kabbah signs a peace agreement with the RUF in November.

1997: Kabbah is ousted by Major-General Paul Koroma, the Armed Forces Revolutionary Council (AFRC), and members of the RUF. Koroma suspends the constitution and bans demonstrations, while Kabbah flees to Guinea.

1998: In February, the Economic Community of West African States Monitoring Group (ECO-

MOG) troops storm Freetown, successfully driving out the rebels. The following month Kabbah returns as president.

1999: In January, RUF rebels retake sections of Freetown from ECOMOG, but are driven out after weeks of brutal fighting. Negotiations in Lomé, Togo, between Kabbah's government and the RUF conclude with a peace agreement in July. Further fighting breaks out within a few months.

2000: In eastern Sierra Leone, UN troops are attacked; British troops arrive in May to Freetown to help evacuate British citizens. Foday Sankoh is captured.

2001: In the spring, UN troops deploy peacefully in rebel-held territory, and disarmament of rebels begins.

2002: With disarmament completed in January, the civil war is considered officially over. Kabbah wins the presidential election held that spring, and his Sierra Leone People's Party (SLPP) wins a majority in parliament.

2003: Foday Sankoh dies of natural causes while awaiting trial for war crimes.

2004: In March, a UN-backed war crimes tribunal begins. In May, first local elections in more than 30 years are held.

2005: The last UN peacekeeping troops depart from Sierra Leone.

2007: In September, Ernest Bai Koroma is sworn in as president of Sierra Leone.

2008: The Special Court for Sierra Leone continues to hold trials related to crimes and actrocities committed during the country's civil war.

2009: Special Court concludes prosecution except for the case against Charles Taylor.

2010: UN Security Council lifts last remaining sanctions against Sierra Leone.

2012: In April Charles Taylor is convicted on 11 charges by the Special Court for Sierra Leone; presidential election scheduled.

FURTHER READING/INTERNET RESOURCES

Beah, Ishmael. *A Long Way Gone: Memoirs of a Boy Soldier.* New York: Farrar, Straus and Giroux, 2007.

Brimson, Samuel. *Sierra Leone-United Arab Emirates (Nations of the World).* Milwaukee, Wis.: World Almanac Library, 2003.

Conrad, David. *Empires of Medieval West Africa: Ghana, Mali, and Songhay (Great Empires of the Past).* New York: Facts on File, 2005.

Habeeb, William Mark. *Civil Wars in Africa (Africa: Progress & Problems).* Philadelphia, Pa.: Mason Crest, 2007.

Levert, Suzanne. *Sierra Leone.* Salt Lake City: Benchmark Books, 2007.

Travel Information

http://www.visitsierraleone.org/
http://www.lonelyplanet.com/sierra-leone
http://travel.state.gov/travel/cis_pa_tw/cis/cis_1016.html

History and Geography

http://www.africa.com/sierra-leone
http://www.sierra-leone.org/Heroes/heroes.html
http://www.cryfreetown.org/history.html

Economic and Political Information

http://news.bbc.co.uk/2/hi/africa/country_profiles/1061561.stm
https://www.cia.gov/library/publications/the-world-factbook/geos/sl.html
http://freetown.usembassy.gov/

Culture and Festivals

http://www.sierra-leone.org/culture.html
http://www.everyculture.com/Sa-Th/Sierra-Leone.html
http://www.traveldocs.com/sl/culture.htm

FOR MORE INFORMATION

Embassy of Sierra Leone
1701 19th Street, NW
Washington, DC 20009
Tel: (202) 939-9261
Fax: (202) 483-1798
Email: info@embassyofsierraleone.net
Website: http://www.embassyofsierraleone.net

U.S. Embassy in Sierra Leone
Leicester Square
Freetown, Sierra Leone
Tel: +232 76 515 000
Fax: +232 76 515 000
Email: consularfreetown@state.gov
Website: http://freetown.usembassy.gov

U.S. Department of State
Bureau of Consular Affairs
2100 Pennsylvania Ave. NW, 4th Floor
Washington, DC 20037
Tel: (202) 736 9130

INDEX

Numbers in **bold italic** refer to captions.

CONTRIBUTORS/PICTURE CREDITS

Professor Robert I. Rotberg is Director of the Program on Intrastate Conflict and Conflict Resolution at the Kennedy School, Harvard University, and President of the World Peace Foundation. He is the author of a number of books and articles on Africa, including *A Political History of Tropical Africa* and *Ending Autocracy, Enabling Democracy: The Tribulations of Southern Africa*.

Judy L. Hasday, a native of Pennsylvania, received a bachelor of arts degree in communications and a master's degree in education in instructional technologies from Temple University, in Philadelphia, Pennsylvania. A certified ophthalmic assistant, Ms. Hasday has written many articles in the field of ophthalmology, as well as dozens of books for young adults. They include New York Public Library "Books for the Teen Age" award winners *James Earl Jones* (1999) and *The Holocaust* (2003). Her book *Extraordinary Women Athletes* was selected as a 2001 Notable Social Studies Trade Book for Young People by the National Social Studies Council. Her free time is devoted to photography, travel, and her pets: cat Sassy and four zebra finches, Scotch, B.J., Atticus, and Jacob.